How to design a
House

How to design a
House

Previous page:
Julius Shulman's iconic
photograph of the Stahl House
(Case Study House #22),
Los Angeles, designed by
Pierre Koenig (1925–2004)
as part of the Case Study
House Program. The
cantilever form of the steel-
framed house was said to
have been suggested by the
client, Buck Stahl.

How to design a House

Introduction

Ask a child to draw a house and what you're likely to get is a box, with squares for windows, an oblong front door, a pointed roof like a triangular hat, a chimney with smoke curling out of it and perhaps some figures lined up alongside – the family who live there. What such representations distil is a powerful archetype. The boundaries of the box declare the house is a unit, a distinct and separate territory. The pitched roof evokes a notion of shelter. The openings for looking out and looking in, for arriving and leaving, signal the fact that the house occupies a specific locality, while the chimney suggests emotional and physical warmth, the focus of hearth and home. 'Home is the place where, when you have to go there, they have to take you in,' said the American poet Robert Frost.

At the same time, children's drawings of houses are similar to schematic depictions of the human face. In dream analysis, the house is often identified as a symbol for the human body. Gaston Bachelard's *La Poétique de l'espace* ('The Poetics of Space' 1958) explores the psychic nature of the house, from the attic where thoughts are kept, corresponding to the superego, to the basement where things are buried and forgotten, the lair of the id. Houses house not only people and their belongings, they also contain memory and meaning. In such domestic theatres, lives are played out.

For architects and designers, the house provides a means to prescribe a way of living as much as a way of expressing more formal or tectonic concerns. 'More a poem than a house, but admirable to live in too,' said the Pre-Raphaelite painter Dante Gabriel Rossetti of Red House, William Morris's (1834–96) home in Kent. Inspired by vernacular and medieval buildings, the shocking simplicity of Red House (as it was then seen) was a step in the direction of Morris's ideal of 'some great room where one talked to one's friends in one corner, and ate in another, and slept in another and worked in another'. An early example of the Arts and Crafts movement's dedication to honesty of construction, Red House would later influence modernist designers in Europe, many of whom learned about it through Hermann Muthesius's seminal book *Das englische Haus* (The English House 1904).

Right: The Rudin House in Leymen, north-eastern France, designed by Herzog & de Meuron in 1997, is described by the architects as a 'heavy and archetypal volume that seems to be suspended above the gentle slope, demonstrating its desire to be perceived as an abstract object'. The pitched roof, tall chimney and large windows are reminiscent of a child's drawing.

Red House, Bexleyheath, Kent was designed by Phillip Webb (1831–1915) and William Morris (1834–96) in the late 1850s. The name of the house was inspired by the red local bricks of which it was constructed. The vernacular style and exposed structural elements had a huge influence on the Arts and Crafts movement. The house was decorated and furnished by Morris and his friends, who included the artists Edward Burne-Jones and Dante Gabriel Rossetti, in a collaborative effort that laid the foundations for the design firm Morris & Co.

Principles

Shelter

All houses provide shelter, but not all shelters are houses. Caves were shelters for early humans, but they are not houses; neither are tents, yurts and other movable dwellings of nomadic peoples. A house implies a specific, settled site, along with some form of self-supporting structure.

The house protects its inhabitants from the elements (or wild animals or marauders) while sheltering the means to sustain life, which for thousands of years meant fire. Whether fire was first brought into primitive huts to warm them, or the hut evolved as a way of enclosing and screening a fire, the two became indivisible. The central open hearth, with smoke escaping through an opening in the roof, persisted from primitive times right through to the medieval hall house and beyond. The subsequent design and location of fireplaces, in part a function of what fuelled them, has had a significant impact on the evolving typology of the house.

Left: The interior of a crofthouse on Flotta, one of the Orkney Islands. One of the central functions of the house from earliest times has been to enclose the fire, the means of sustaining life.

Right: These cliff-houses at Mesa Verde, Colorado, which date from the twelfth century, were constructed by the Pueblo people, who had long settled the area. The rectangular rooms were used as either dwellings or storerooms.

Kiva.L

Left: *The Interior of a House in Delft* (1658) by the Dutch painter Pieter de Hooch (1629–84), a contemporary of Vermeer. Like Vermeer, de Hooch often painted quiet domestic scenes. The notion of the house as an intimate space for a family began in the Netherlands. This painting, which shows a rear courtyard with a passageway leading through to the street, makes a clear distinction between the public and private worlds.

What we understand today by shelter has a further implication of refuge and privacy. Houses are where we retreat from our public lives, where we can relax and be our true selves. They are places of stability, belonging and identity, of psychological as much as physical comfort. The house is where environment is tamed, domesticated and made personal.

This has not always been the case. Early households were more akin to loosely knit communities, where familial ties were not necessarily pre-eminent. In the Middle Ages, and right up to the seventeenth century, many houses also served as workshops or places of business, accommodating as many as two dozen people. (A study of census records in poor urban areas reveals an equivalent density right up to the end of the nineteenth century, with whole families in single rooms.) Privacy was unknown and even sleeping was communal.

Social historians trace the beginning of the domestic interior to the bourgeois households of seventeenth-century Holland, where the house was first conceived as a separate, special place for a family – an intimacy recorded in the paintings of Vermeer, de Witte and de Hooch. 'The home of the home is the Netherlands,' architectural critic and theorist Philip Tabor has written. Owing to Dutch domination of trade and finance during that period, it was a notion that soon spread. Space was increasingly separated into daytime and night-time uses, and the beginning of corridors or separate circulation spaces replaced the order arrangement in which one room simply led to another. Previously, in grand houses or palaces, the axial progress from anteroom to inner chamber to seat of power – the *enfilade* – was a progress of state; more ordinarily, interconnecting rooms muddled everyone up together.

Merchant houses in Amsterdam. By the seventeenth century, Amsterdam was the wealthiest city in the world and a financial and trading centre. The architect Philips Vingboons (c1607–78) was responsible for the distinctive version of classicism that arose in Amsterdam during this period. A key characteristic was the 'neck front', or *halsgevel,* façade, adapted to the typically narrow city plots.

Function

What else do houses do, aside from providing us with a roof over our heads? At the very least, we expect them to facilitate the performance of everyday activities – cooking, eating, bathing and sleeping – and to provide a framework within which these activities can take place comfortably and effectively. Their function consists, in a sense, of being fit for such purposes.

Early modernist architects viewed such functionalism in a mechanistic sense: 'One can be proud of having a house as serviceable as a typewriter,' said Le Corbusier (1887–1965). In *Vers une architecture* ('Toward an Architecture' 1923) he wrote:

> Eradicate from your mind any hard and fast conceptions in regard to the dwelling house and look at the question from an objective and critical angle, and you will inevitably arrive at the 'House-Tool', the mass-production house, available for everyone, incomparably healthier than the old kind (and morally so too) and beautiful in the same sense that the working tools, familiar to us in our present existence, are beautiful.

Up until the early twentieth century, and for even longer in some parts of the world, most households, even relatively humble ones, depended on servants to perform domestic duties. By the nineteenth century this had led to a clear distinction in spatial planning between public areas where guests could be received, private rooms where they couldn't, and 'below stairs' or utility areas that were the preserve of the staff and which might never be visited by those who employed them. During the same period rooms were increasingly ascribed specific functions, often along the lines of gender and age, as well as class: night nurseries, day nurseries, morning rooms, libraries, pantries, sculleries and so on.

The disappearance of the servant class, which began to trickle away between the world wars, along with the introduction of technological improvements (electricity, indoor plumbing, central

Right: Villa Mairea (1938–41) in Noormarkku, Turku, Finland, was designed by Alvar Aalto (1898–1976) for the art patrons and co-founders of Artek, Harry and Maire Gullichsen. The free flow of space at different levels, the merging of the house with its idyllic woodland setting, and the use of natural materials are all characteristic of Scandinavian modernism. The central double columns, which help to support the upper floor, are clad in rattan.

heating) and the invention of labour-saving appliances, signalled the beginning of a gradual shift from a hierarchical approach to the layout of domestic space. By the 1960s it was no longer unthinkable for people to eat and entertain in the kitchen; by the end of the century separate dining rooms had all but disappeared. Morris's 'one great room' – which in his case was a nostalgic hankering after the inclusiveness of the medieval hall house – was reborn in the form of multifunctional, open-plan space.

If the house as a shelter keeps intruders at bay, another of its key functions is to serve as a container or repository – inclusion as opposed to exclusion. Up until the eighteenth century most people owned little more than could be stored in a simple chest. Furniture types were similarly limited. With the rise of a middle class and increased leisure, types of belongings and furniture began to proliferate, even though it was by no means uncommon for people in the eighteenth century to rent most of what they used on a daily basis. By contrast, the average house today contains an astonishing quantity and variety of *types* of things – from pasta makers and dishwashers to ski boots and hedge-trimmers – and is largely defined by the way such possessions are organized.

Left: The smooth running of large Victorian and Edwardian households depended on an army of servants 'below stairs'. Internal planning was often dictated by the need to maintain a separation between servants' quarters and functional spaces such as kitchens on the one hand, and family or public rooms on the other.

Right: Crescent House in Wiltshire, designed for his own use by the British architect Ken Shuttleworth (1952–) in 1999–2000, takes the form of two nesting crescents. The inner crescent is extensively glazed to make a seamless connection with the garden.

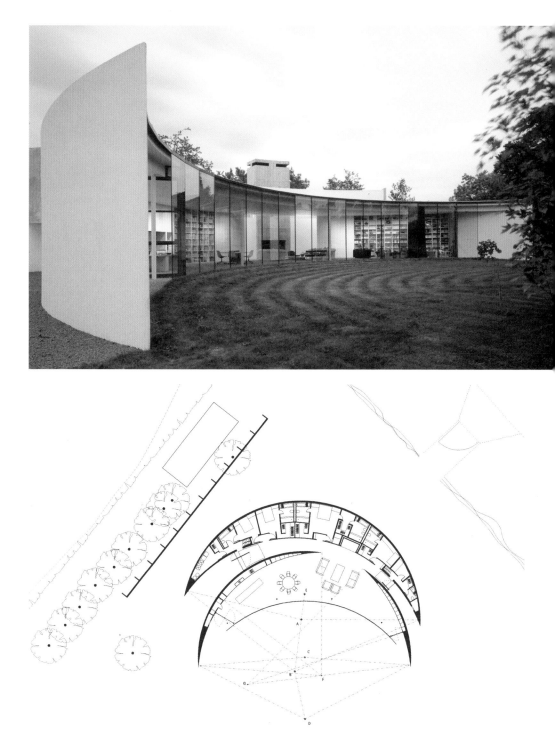

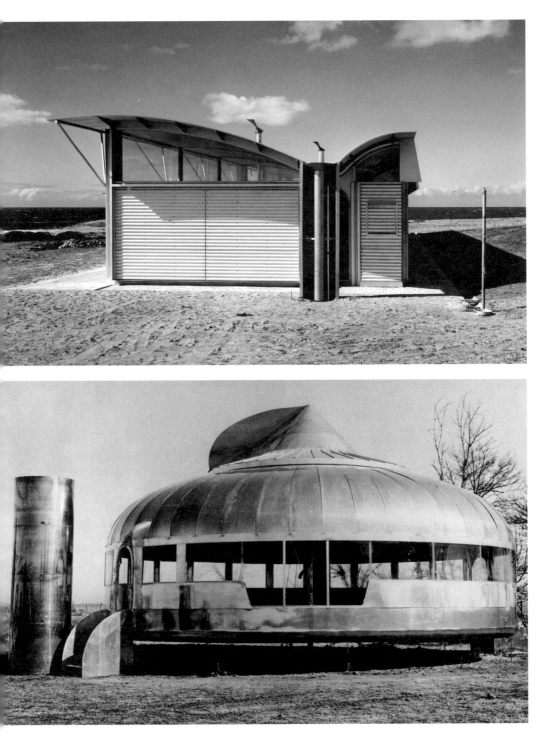

20

Left above: The Magney House, Bingie Point, New South Wales, was designed in 1982–4 by Glenn Murcutt (1936–). Oriented to capture the north light, the house makes use of many passive strategies to control interior temperature and maximize energy efficiency, including slatted blinds and insulation. The asymmetric V-shaped roof collects rainwater for recycling. Murcutt's buildings show an acute sensitivity to site and nature.

Left below: Philosopher, inventor, architect, engineer and teacher Buckminster Fuller (1895–1983) dedicated his life to devising solutions for buildings and transport that could be mass-produced using the simplest and most sustainable means, decades before saving energy and resources became a major preoccupation. His Wichita House or 'Dymaxion Dwelling Machine' was a lightweight, full-size family house intended for mass production, developed with the Beech Aircraft Company of Wichita in Kansas.

Servicing arrangements – lines of supply – mean that, over the years, houses have increasingly served as *consumers*, hooked up to networks that deliver power, fuel and water. Yet in the future it looks likely that houses will need to perform as *generators*, or at least conservators and collectors, micro-efficient cogs in a much wider strategy for managing finite resources. In Archipelago House (2000) by New York-born British architect Seth Stein, located on a remote island in the Finnish Archipelago, solar technology is built into the design, with the building grid informed by the dimensions of a standard photovoltaic panel, 12 of which are mounted on the roof edge. The work of Australian architect Glenn Murcutt (1936–) shows a similar sensitivity, combining elements of a rural vernacular and a restrained modernism with a finely tuned response to local conditions.

Expression

The UK television game show *Through the Keyhole*, in which panellists are shown a video tour of a famous person's house and then invited to guess that person's identity, is based on the simple premise that the way we decorate and furnish our houses provides clues to lifestyle and personality. When we are invited into someone's home, and study the titles on the bookshelves or the objects on the mantelpiece, we are playing the same social game. Yet what people display in their houses can be more revealing of aspiration than actuality – as in, say, a state-of-the-art range cooker in the kitchen where most meals are microwaved.

Taste and status have long been embodied in houses; individuality less so. The manifestations of power, prestige and wealth are built into the fabric of great houses, from the fortified castles of the Normans to the mansions of Victorian magnates. Late seventeenth-century France introduced the notion of a decorative unity, in which soft furnishings in particular spelled out a harmonious composition. The classically inspired architects and designers of the eighteenth century transformed ordinary townhouses into models of order, symmetry and elegance.

The notion that a house should be a vehicle for individual taste and preference dates from a time much closer to the present day. Ever since architects emerged as a professional class distinct from master builders, which began to happen during the Renaissance, there has been potential for conflict between the designer of a house and the person or people for whom it is designed. How far should an architect dictate how a house should be used, furnished and decorated? In 1938, when Sir Edwin Lutyens (1869–1944) returned to New Delhi to oversee repairs and restore the original decorations of the Viceroy's House, which he had handed over some ten years previously, he was dismayed to discover many unsympathetic alterations made by a subsequent vicereine, Lady Willingdon – the sort of person, he said, who would put a bay window in the Parthenon. Le Corbusier's relationships with many of his clients were famously strained (an early house he designed for his parents in 1912, the Villa Jeanneret-Perret, otherwise known as the Maison Blanche, brought them to the brink of financial ruin). When a client complained to Frank Lloyd Wright (1867–1959) that the dining room ceiling was leaking, the architect's advice was to move the chairs.

Whose house is it anyway?

Below and right: Soft and Hairy House (1994), by the Tokyo partnership Ushida Findlay, was designed and built for a young couple in Tsukuba City near Tokyo. Taking the concept of 'inside-out' living to its extreme, the house consists of a fusion of sensual organic forms. The large roof garden extends the metaphor of 'house as organism' while providing a degree of insulation.

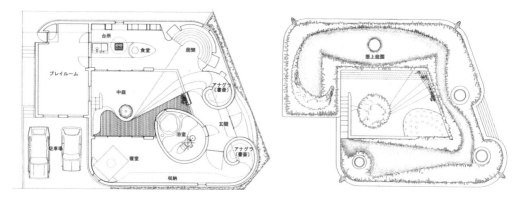

23

A common practice in many areas where winter is extreme, the principle of 'earth-sheltering' was adopted in the design of this house in Wales by Future Systems. The site of the house is on the fringes of a national park: earth-sheltering also enables minimal disruption to the surrounding landscape.

Process

Blueprint

A house is a negotiation of space, and the first space where that negotiation takes place is in the mind. Whatever else informs design – site specifics, structural possibilities, a client's brief – capturing thought is the start.

Do architects draw the building or build the drawing? It was not until the Renaissance, when perspective was first understood, that the two-dimensional page was trusted as a means of conveying three-dimensional reality. That coincided with the beginning of printing and the wider availability of paper, which meant that for the first time drawings could be a means of disseminating ideas. As Jonathan Hill has pointed out in *Immaterial Architecture* (2006), drawing as a means of generating ideas began to make a distinction between architects or designers as conceptualists, and master builders whose expertise was largely derived from built examples and previous practice (what one might call a hands-on approach):

> The [modern] architect and the architectural drawing are twins… the drawing is the key that unlocked the status of the architect and other visual artists. Associated with visual rather than manual labour, the new status of the drawing and the architect increased the status of the building.

Drawing and writing have continued to be as important as building for many architects. As Frank Lloyd Wright once caustically observed of Le Corbusier: 'Well, now that he's finished one building, he'll go write four books about it.'

From the back-of-the-envelope scribble that records a fleeting moment of inspiration, to the computer-generated detail or working drawing that provides specific information for constructors, the architectural drawing (or model) serves diverse purposes. Sir Edwin Lutyens's effortless handling of classical proportions, such as the golden section and ratios based on the Fibonacci

Right: *House* (1993) by British artist Rachel Whiteread was a concrete cast of the interior of a Victorian terraced house in East London. Exhibited at the location of the original house, 193 Grove Road, the sculpture played with perceptions of interior space – fireplaces protruded, door knobs became recesses. *House* won the Turner Prize in 1993 and was demolished by Tower Hamlets Council in 1994.

28

Left: This colour rendering of Frank Lloyd Wright's K C DeRhodes House in South Bend, Indiana (1906) set a style of presentational drawing that became identified with Wright's work. The drawing, however, with its sepia outlines and soft colour washes, was the work of Marion Mahony (1871–1961), who was employed in Wright's studio. Mahony was one of the first women in the world to be licensed as an architect and only the second to graduate from MIT. Wright acknowledged her contribution by pencilling on the drawing: 'Drawn by Mahony after FLW and Hiroshige'.

Right below: Mies van der Rohe's drawing style, by contrast, was impressionistic, minimal but suggestive.

sequence (0:1:1:2:3:5:8…) enabled him to marry symmetrical frontages with asymmetrical plans, and has been linked to his preference for using ⅛-inch squared graph paper. By contrast, Mies van der Rohe's (1886–1968) drawing style was minimal and suggestive, the omissions 'cognitive as well as spatial', as Jonathan Hill points out.

Presentational material, often highly rendered elevations or intricate models, might be seen as selling tools, promoting a scheme to a client, or as a demonstration of an architect's worldview. Frank Lloyd Wright, who was a voracious collector of Japanese *ukiyo-e* woodblock prints, and a particular admirer of the work of Hiroshige, adopted the same flattened graphic style in his presentation drawings, down to the square red colophon that was his signature or seal. Many architects have also been artists. In Charles Rennie Mackintosh's (1868–1928) watercolours one can detect the same synthesis of natural and graphic form that was evident in his architectural designs.

Ever since the birth of the Modern Movement, it has been accepted that the plan, or the functional disposition of space to serve human requirements, is what dictates the external appearance of the house. The idea of the plan as a generator has had far-reaching implications on design.

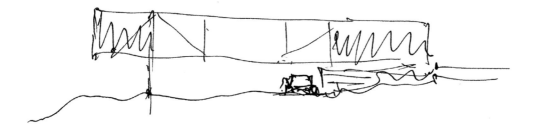

Site

'No house should ever be on a hill or on anything. It should be of the hill. Belonging to it. Hill and house should live together, each the happier for the other,' said Frank Lloyd Wright in 1932. Fallingwater (1935–9), arguably Wright's masterpiece, achieves such a unity, its tiered horizontal concrete slabs dramatically cantilevered over a waterfall – at once an abstraction of its setting and an integral part of it.

One of the greatest exponents of an organic approach to architecture, Wright designed many of his buildings as expressions of their particular sites, both literally and metaphorically. The long low lines of his 'Prairie Houses' (1900–17) echoed the flat grasslands that surrounded them. Taliesin West (1937) in Arizona was built from local stone combined with concrete made out of local aggregate, so that the structure appeared to grow out of its rocky desert setting. According to Wright, 'Organic buildings are the strength and lightness of the spiders' spinning, buildings qualified by light, bred by native character to environment, married to the ground.'

Right: Fallingwater (1935–9), Frank Lloyd Wright's most famous building, under construction. House and site are closely integrated, with concrete floor slabs cantilevered over a waterfall.

Left below: The Darwin D. Martin House (1903–5) in Buffalo, New York, is widely considered to be the most important design of the first half of Frank Lloyd Wright's career and the finest of his Prairie Houses. Wright's aim was to reduce the number of separate rooms and to create a unity of space through the free flow of air, light and views.

Left: 'Span' houses, developments built between 1948 and 1969 largely around London and south-east England, were designed by British architect Eric Lyons (1912–80), often in collaboration with landscape architect Ivor Cunningham (1928–2007). Lyons, a modernist influenced by Walter Gropius, was dedicated to a clear, contemporary style. Equally radical was the arrangement of the estates around shared landscapes in order to foster a sense of community.

Right below: This 1970 photograph of a loft in New York's SoHo shows an early manifestation of the trend for setting up home in redundant commercial and industrial buildings.

While houses can be shaped and defined by their settings – 'married to the ground' – they can also be the means of exploring settings. Mies van der Rohe's Farnsworth House (1951) in Illinois, designed as a weekend retreat in woodland on the banks of a river, is a glass box suspended from a steel frame, the floor raised up over ground level. The house is both an architectural object placed in a landscape and a means of framing a landscape pictorially. 'If you view nature through the glass walls of the Farnsworth House,' said Mies, 'it gains a more profound significance than if viewed from outside. That way more is said about nature – it becomes part of a larger whole.' The development of plate-glass and steel-frame construction at the beginning of the twentieth century opened up new possibilities for houses to merge with their sites, allowing interior space to flow into the exterior so that the boundaries between the two were blurred.

More prosaically, a site presents a number of specific physical parameters that must be accommodated or overcome. Underlying soil conditions will dictate the nature and structure of foundations. The size and shape of the plot may place limitations on the size and shape of the plan. Orientation, slope, climatic conditions,

Below: Mies van der Rohe's Farnsworth House (1951) stands in woodland on the banks of a river and was designed as a weekend retreat. An exquisite architectural object placed in a landscape, it is also a means of framing a landscape pictorially.

neighbouring buildings, existing trees and other factors will all have a bearing on design, as will local planning regulations and zoning laws. Even in the middle of nowhere, a site is no blank slate.

In some cases, house and site are one and the same thing. In urban areas, where the greater proportion of the housing stock is decades old and plots are scarce and prohibitively expensive, buying a period property and gutting it is one way of creating a new house within an existing shell or footprint. This was the approach adopted by Richard Rogers (1933–) in the design of his own house, a Victorian townhouse in London's Chelsea, whose soaring double-height internal spaces, with an open kitchen placed prominently on the ground floor, are not the spatial arrangement that the traditional façade would lead you to expect. Such strategies are also evident in the conversion of non-domestic buildings – redundant factories and warehouses, for example, decommissioned churches and chapels, old schools and barns – in what one might call the 'loft aesthetic'.

Site is also context in a broader sense. What's outside the front door? A road, a lawn, a driveway? Houses are the building blocks of streets, suburbs, towns and cities, woven into countless patterns of habitation.

Maison à Bordeaux (1998) was designed by OMA (Office for Metropolitan Architecture), a practice founded by Rem Koolhaas (1944–) in 1975. This private house on a hill overlooking Bordeaux consists of three levels, the lowest a series of intimate caverns carved out of the hill, the ground floor a glass room that merges with the landscape, and the top floor split between areas for the parents and the children. Central to the design is a 'machine' – a 3 x 3.5 metre elevator platform that rises up through the levels.

The client, who had been seriously injured in a car accident and was a wheelchair user, wanted a 'complex' house because it would define his immediate world. The platform allows him to access and explore his surroundings.

Left: In the days before fast and efficient transportation links, vernacular houses were generally built with what lay to hand. This cottage in the Orkney Islands is constructed out of stone cleared from the land. Peat or sod roofs were also typical.

Right below: Simple frame structures infilled with woven panels of fibre are raised up on stilts in an area prone to flooding.

Structure, material and form

For centuries there were two basic types of house structure. In the frame-and-panel method, a load-bearing skeleton or frame, usually of wood, was erected and the spaces filled in with panels or some other sort of material. The other method was to construct walls out of a large number of small units, such as bricks or blocks of stone. A variation on that theme, and perhaps the most ancient of all building techniques, was earthen construction, where load-bearing walls were shaped from rammed earth, cob, or cut sods of turf. Structure has an intimate relationship with material. Centuries ago, when transportation was difficult, vernacular houses were built with what lay to hand: wood in areas where timber was plentiful, stone where stone could be cleared from the land.

Timber

In medieval Europe, timber building was cheapest, fastest and easiest to work, and many houses of the period were constructed on the frame-and-panel principle, with the infill panels often consisting of wattle and daub. Timber building remained dominant until stocks of native hardwoods (under pressure from shipbuilding but chiefly charcoal burning) began to decline in the sixteenth century. Evidence of a certain cross-fertilization of skills was apparent – many medieval timber roofs with their massive beams and trusses resemble ships' hulls turned upside down. While timber building began to give way to masonry construction in Europe, elsewhere – in Scandinavia, North America, China and Japan, for example – the tradition of building in wood persisted.

Left below: Timber construction has long been prevalent in North America. This timber-clad timber-framed eighteenth-century Colonial house is in Westbrook, Connecticut.

Right: The *machiya*, or timber-framed merchant house, is an example of traditional Japanese vernacular architecture closely associated with Kyoto. Typical features of the street frontages are tiled roofs and wooden lattices.

Right below: The *machiya* form is typically long and thin, incorporating one or two internal courtyard gardens, or *tsuboniwa*. Sliding paper screens, or *shoji*, partition interior spaces and separate outdoors from in.

Paper House (1995), Lake Yamanaka, Yamanashi, Japan, was designed by Shigeru Ban (1957–), a pioneer of paper tube structures. This house was the first in which paper tubes were authorized for structural use. More than a hundred paper tubes define the interior and exterior spaces.

Left above: Hadrian's Villa (Villa Adriana), a summer retreat in Tivoli for the Roman emperor Hadrian, was constructed in the early second century AD and comprised more than 30 buildings. The villa displays detailing taken from a number of ancient and classical orders and includes a pool (the Canopus) surrounded by statuary and columns and an artificial grotto and temple (the Serapeum).

Left below: Place des Vosges is the oldest square in Paris and the prototype for subsequent European residential squares. It was built between 1605 and 1612, probably to designs by Baptiste du Cerceau (c1545–90). The influence of classicism is evident in its symmetries, with individual houses united in a continuous façade constructed of red brick with stone facings.

Masonry

Stone, at first reserved for more monumental structures such as churches and cathedrals, or for fortified buildings such as castles, found a new role when classical ideals of architecture were rediscovered in Renaissance Italy and gradually spread northward. Unlike timber building, which naturally tends to be more adaptable but also haphazard, constructing houses from repetitive and regularly shaped and scaled elements, whether brick or stone, lends itself to symmetry and order.

The Renaissance represented a profound break from the Gothic: classicism was seen as the pure expression of the order and proportion of the natural world, with the human being at its centre. Leonardo da Vinci's *Vitruvian Man* (c1487) is a famous representation of such concepts. Leon Battista Alberti's (1404–72) Palazzo Rucellai, built in Florence between 1446 and the 1450s, was the first attempt to apply the classical orders to an exterior elevation and was the result of intense studies into the rules of perspective and proportion. The shallow modelling of pilasters on the façade clearly delineates three separate stories: the rusticated lower, or ground, floor; the first floor, or *piano nobile*, housing the public apartments, and the attic storey above.

The most influential of all Italian Renaissance architects, however, was Andrea Palladio (1508–80). Originally trained as a mason, Palladio had studied the classical ruins in Rome at first hand and produced a number of exquisite villas in the countryside near Vicenza in the mid-sixteenth century. The Villa Capra, nicknamed 'La Rotonda' (designed 1566), a square building with a domed central hall and a portico on each of the four faces, was hugely influential, particularly in England, as was his compendious study *I quattro libri dell'architettura* ('The Four Books of Architecture') in which Palladio set out his observations. Other influential texts of the period included Vitruvius's architectural treatise, *De architectura* ('On Architecture'), written in the first century BC but first published in 1486.

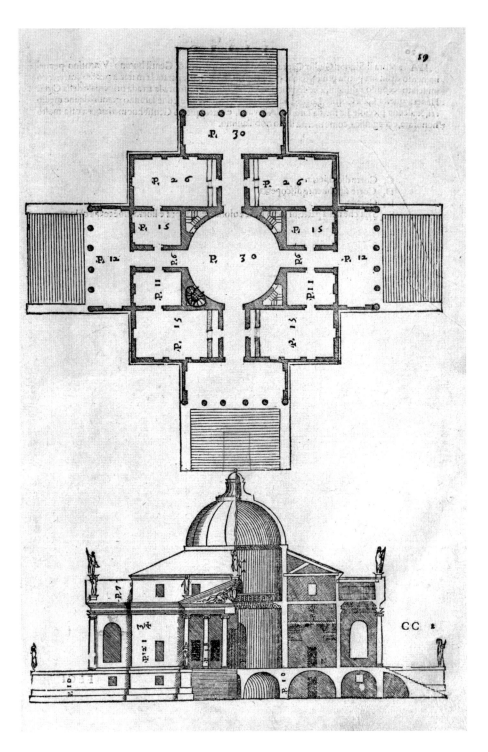

Inigo Jones (1573–1652), described by Nikolaus Pevsner as 'the first English architect in the modern sense', absorbed Palladian ideals at first hand when he travelled to Italy with his patron, the Earl of Arundel. The Queen's House in Greenwich, designed by Jones in 1616 and completed in the 1630s, is the first entirely classical building in Britain.

Early patrons of the classical style were almost exclusively well-travelled members of the aristocracy or landed gentry, such as Lord Burlington, whose Chiswick House (1726–9) was directly inspired by the Palladian villas. But the rise of Palladianism also coincided with a boom in urban development. Shortage of timber had already seen brick replace wood as the principal building material in England (particularly after the Great Fire obliterated medieval London in 1666). Glass had improved in both size and transparency, and the introduction of the sliding sash at the end of the seventeenth century gave façades a lighter and more sparkling appearance. Whether constructed in brick or stone, Georgian terraces, laid out in neat grids and punctuated by squares or circuses, incorporated classicism into a pattern of ordinary building. The Royal Crescent in Bath (1767–75), designed by John Wood the Younger (1728–82), unites individual townhouses in a sweeping Ionic parade. During the latter half of the eighteenth century, building regulations came into force that divided domestic building into four classes, defined by size, construction and position. First-floor apartments were the most important and were announced on the façade with the tallest and most ornamented windows. Windows higher up became progressively smaller and squarer, while the ground floor was often given a rusticated treatment in imitation of Renaissance buildings.

Elements of such underlying classical proportions remained in nineteenth-century domestic architecture, although much of the finesse was missing. Classicism, however, was but one style among many, and rampant ornamentation, from varying sources and increasingly mass-produced, embellished houses inside and out. In Britain, the spread of the railway saw an explosion of house-building, much of it taking the form of brick terraces. A rising middle class created an expanding market for household goods, while the long reach of the British Empire, along with improved communications, helped to promote a conformity of taste around the world. The home, if not actually a castle, could always have the trappings of one.

'Masses of sordidness, filth and squalor, embroidered with pompous and vulgar hideousness,' was William Morris's condemnation of the products of the Industrial Revolution. Influenced by Ruskin and other theorists of the mid-century Gothic Revival, Morris was inspired to formulate a design approach based on constructional honesty. At Red House and later houses of the Arts and Crafts movement, exposed beams, brick arches and plain distempered walls displayed themselves for what they were, while allowing the structure of the house to be read.

Left: The Queen's House, Greenwich (1616–35), designed by Inigo Jones, is the first fully classical building in England.

Right: The 'Tulip Stairs' at the Queen's House: the first centrally unsupported spiral stair in Britain.

Left and left below: Villa
Savoye (1928–30) at Poissy,
near Paris, designed by
Le Corbusier, clearly
expresses his 'Five Points
of Architecture', which he
enumerated in 1926: the use
of pillars or 'piloti' to raise
houses above the ground;
the free interior layout or
plan; the free façade,
made possible by the
independence of structural
frame and exterior walls;
ribbon windows; and the flat
roof terrace, providing a
connection with nature and
replacing the site area.

Reinforced concrete

It was some time after the Industrial Revolution that new structural
systems became possible. While the Romans had been the first to
make concrete and use it structurally to create domes and vaults,
that knowledge was lost with the fall of the Roman Empire (AD 476)
and it was not until the nineteenth century that concrete was
rediscovered and its potential re-explored. French engineers and
architects were first to grasp the principle of reinforcing concrete
with metal rods or wire mesh to give it the strength to span greater
distances. 'Steel concrete' or 'ferro-concrete' was patented by
François Hennebique (1842–1941) in the 1890s and first used in
the construction of the Weaver Flour Mill in Swansea, Wales, in
1897 (demolished 1984). Auguste Perret (1874–1954) was another
architect to exploit the new material. Perret's architectural office,
located in his landmark concrete-frame building in Paris, 25bis rue
Franklin (1902–4), was where the young Le Corbusier came to
work in 1908.

Reinforced concrete, unlike traditional construction materials such
as timber or masonry, permitted freedom of form. For the first time,
a structural framework could become a unified whole. Because
walls were not load-bearing, they could be pierced by openings in
any arrangement. Windows could be continuous, ribbon-like or
vertical, to maximize light in the interior or to announce internal
volumes and spatial arrangement on the façade. Framed
construction meant that floor plans could be open and flexibly
divided to provide a flow of space. The entire relationship between
house and site could be inverted, with the garden shifted onto the
flat roof and the house itself raised on slender columns, or pilotis,
so that it hovered over the ground.

One of Le Corbusier's most significant early houses was Maison
La Roche, designed for Raoul La Roche, a banker who was also a
collector of avant-garde art (part of the project was a contiguous
but separate house for Le Corbusier's brother, Albert Jeanneret,
now the home of the Fondation Le Corbusier). Completed in 1925,

Left: Villa Sarabhai in Ahmedabad, Gujarat, designed by Le Corbusier in the mid-1950s, has a turfed roof, with a chute that spills water down into a paradise-like garden pool.

Left below: The interior of Villa Sarabhai features a series of tile-lined vaults and planes of strong colour, a significant departure from Le Corbusier's earlier 'white villas'.

Right: Unité d'Habitation (completed in 1953) at Marseille was Le Corbusier's solution to the problem of mass housing, and became one of the most influential buildings of the postwar era. Housing 1,600 people in 23 different apartment types, the building was animated by communal life and includes a shopping centre, hotel, restaurant and post office as well as a gymnasium, pool and crèche. The façades of the building are strongly modelled, with openings set back to exclude the hot summer sun.

the house occupies a tight, awkward site at the edge of the
sixteenth arrondissement of Paris. The exterior is stark and plain,
its pure white walls graphically contrasted with black-framed ribbon
windows; inside is what Charles Jencks has described as 'one of
the first great sequences of space in Modern architecture'. As well
as being a collector, La Roche liked to entertain, and accordingly
Le Corbusier provided a curved ramped gallery leading off the
triple-height entrance where paintings could be hung and parties
held. An interior balcony and bridge and intersecting double- and
triple-height spaces created an entirely new sense of movement,
not merely a free or open plan, but a free *flow* of space.

While the house for Le Corbusier was famously a *machine à
habiter* ('machine for living in'), he was not saying, as some of his
critics later argued, that the house was *only* a machine, but that its
primary purpose was to serve modern needs. Contemporary
photographs of Le Corbusier's early machines for living generally
featured a machine for driving parked outside – the architect's way
of hammering the point home. What is instructive about these
posed photographs today is how innovative and modern the
buildings still look and how antique the cars.

The private villas that secured Le Corbusier his international
reputation as the leading modernist architect by the end of the
1920s were essentially one-offs, designed for and commissioned
by well-to-do people. Yet a key aim for Le Corbusier, as much as
for progressive designers of the Bauhaus, was to develop a mass-
produced housing 'type' to meet the demands for social housing
after World War I. An early attempt at Pessac, a suburb of
Bordeaux, did not prove cost-effective. More successful was the
prototype for mass housing Le Corbusier designed after the next
world war, when Europe faced reconstruction on a massive scale.
This was the Unité d'Habitation ('Housing Unit') in Marseille, which
was completed in 1952 and became one of the most influential
buildings of the postwar era.

Built by default of reinforced concrete (steel was prohibitively expensive in Europe at the time), the Unité expressed Le Corbusier's notions of social and urban planning and enshrined his new proportional system, the 'Modulor', which had a clear basis in da Vinci's *Vitruvian Man*. Housing 1,600 people in 23 different apartment types, the building was animated by communal life: a shopping centre, comprising a hotel, restaurant, post office, pharmacy, bakery and food shops, occupied the seventh and eighth floors. The rooftop was a recreation area, while other facilities included a gymnasium, pool and crèche. A model of the way great architecture can integrate the individual and the social, sadly its achievement was rarely equalled by imitations that sprang up in its wake.

Steel and glass

Reinforced concrete was not the only new material to make an impact on architectural form at the beginning of the twentieth century. Developments in iron production and the emergence of steel saw the frame-and-panel structural system revisited with striking consequences – one of which was the skyscraper or high-rise, the first all-American building type.

While iron was not a new material, its use in buildings had previously been limited. At the end of the eighteenth century, new methods of smelting iron with coke increased its quality and led to an expansion in the market. Cast-iron structural members began to be used, first in bridges, then in early factories. Because there were no precedents for such construction, the profiles and strengths of individual elements had to be precisely calculated, inaugurating an ongoing collaboration between engineers and architects that still underpins contemporary design.

After fire devastated the centre of Chicago in 1871, it was noted that exposed cast-iron beams and columns had melted, whereas those encased in masonry had not. Effective fire-proofing paved the way for the first high-rise buildings in Chicago and New York,

Right above: Maison de Verre (1928–32) in Paris, designed by Pierre Chareau (1883–1950) and Bernard Bijvoet (1889–1979), displays an early modernist use of industrial materials such as steel, glass blocks and perforated metal. The façade is infilled with translucent glass blocks interspersed with clear glass panes.

Right below: Philip Johnson's (1906–2005) Glass House (1949) at New Canaan, Connecticut, which he built for his own use, is an essay in transparency and minimalism. The only floor-to-ceiling partition in the otherwise open interior is the brick cylindrical structure that encloses the bathroom.

Originally constructed as the German Pavilion for the 1929 International Exposition in Barcelona, Mies van der Rohe's radical design demonstrated new spatial possibilities, particularly in the relationship between the interior and exterior. His Barcelona chair was designed especially for the pavilion. Demolished only a year later, the pavilion was reconstructed in the early 1980s.

Left: Exterior and interior
of the Kaufmann Desert
House (1946), Palm Springs,
California, one of the most
famous houses designed by
Richard Neutra. The client,
Edgar Kaufmann, had
commissioned Frank Lloyd
Wright to design Fallingwater
ten years previously. This
vacation house, with its flat
roofs and strong horizontal
planes, and large sliding
glass walls, was conceived
as a pavilion and was closely
integrated into the desert
landscape. According to
Neutra: 'Exacting attention
has to be paid to our intricate
sensory world.'

in which all the structural loads were carried by metal frameworks clad in masonry. Emblematic of the revolutionary new American architecture was the work of Louis Sullivan (1856–1924).

Steel – perhaps the definitive structural material of the twentieth century – was developed in the late nineteenth century in response to a demand for a material stronger than iron. Within decades, steel-framed towers loomed over the streets of Chicago and Manhattan, although early examples rarely expressed a steel aesthetic. It was early modernists such as Mies van der Rohe and Walter Gropius (1883–1969) who partnered the steel frame with plate glass to forge a new architectural language. In the 1920s, new processes enabled plate glass to be produced economically in large sizes and with full transparency. Mies's German Pavilion, designed for the 1929 Barcelona Universal Exposition, a glass house minimally supported by a steel framework, shocked contemporaries with its abstraction and dematerialization.

The altered relationship between a building and its surroundings permitted by the use of glass and steel was not simply an outcome of structural development. Many architects in the early decades of the twentieth century were inspired and influenced by traditional Japanese houses, which enshrined a very different approach to space. Japan had been a closed society for 250 years when an intervention by the US Navy in the mid-nineteenth century forced it to open up to the rest of the world. Once trade had become established, the West was exposed to Japanese art and artifacts and a craze for japonaiserie followed. An early American traveller to Japan was Edward Morse, who wrote the widely read and highly influential *Japanese Homes and Their Surroundings*, published in 1886. This text, accompanied by Morse's sketches, was the first to introduce Western readers to Japanese ways of living.

Charles Rennie Mackintosh, Walter Gropius, Marcel Breuer (1902–81) and Frank Lloyd Wright were among the many architects influenced by Japanese art, culture and architecture. Centuries before modernism, the Japanese had already been building timber-frame houses with non-load bearing walls, flexible planning and a heightened connection between interior and exterior spaces. In the traditional *shoin-zukuri* house, *fusuma* – sliding paper-covered screens – modulated the transition from outside to inside and from room to room, while the dimensions of the *tatami* floor mat provided a module for spatial design. Few areas were assigned single functions, and furniture, including rolled mattresses for sleeping, was brought out only when needed. The flexibility of such houses was a direct inspiration for the modern open plan, and their contemplative focus on the shifting quality of light and shadow served as a clear demonstration that less could be more.

Prefabrication

The Case Study House Program, launched in 1945 by the California-based magazine *Arts & Architecture* (1938–67), was a progressive venture aimed at addressing social needs through modern design. Eight houses were commissioned from a number of architects, with the idea that these might serve as prototypes for inexpensive housing. Among those invited to produce designs were Richard Neutra (1892–1970), Pierre Koenig (Julius Shulman's iconic photograph of Koenig's Case Study House #22 appears at the beginning of this book) and Charles Eames (1907–78).

Eames's own house, Case Study House #8 (1949), which he designed in collaboration with his wife Ray (1912–88), was a steel-frame structure that made a radical and economical use of prefabricated industrial components. Although a great deal of research (sponsored by major American steel producers) had gone into prefabrication before the war, the Eames House was the first prefabricated house to win acclaim. Designed as two linked rectangular structures, one a studio and one the living quarters, it achieved maximum volume with a minimum of materials. The structural shell took five men just 16 hours to erect, while the roof deck was completed by one man over a period of three days. The colourful façade, the strong yet minimal steel frame, the flexible partitioning, the fluid relationship between indoors and

Right: Koshino House by the Japanese architect Tadao Ando (1941–) was designed in 1979–80 and completed in two stages. It consists of two parallel wings, half buried in the landscape, joined by an underground passage that leads to a central courtyard. Many of the elements most characteristic of Ando's work are in evidence here: the use of concrete to give a strong sense of materiality, the play of light and shadow, and the free flow of air.

Left: Case Study House #8 (1949), better known as the Eames House, was designed by Charles and Ray Eames as part of the Case Study House Program. Comprising two linked steel-framed structures, one the living quarters and the other the studio, the design made radical use of prefabricated industrial components.

outdoors achieved through sliding doors and windows: all this fused together references to Mondrian and De Stijl, the Miesian machine aesthetic and traditional Japanese architecture in a modest and harmonious whole. 'The house must make no insistent demands for itself, but rather aid as background for life in work,' was part of the brief the Eameses set themselves.

None of the other early Case Study Houses used prefabricated elements, and most relied on simple wood-frame structures, with infill panels made of a range of economical materials. One of the most commercially successful was Levitt and Sons' 'Cape Codder', which sold for $5,000 and rapidly proliferated in 'Levittowns' across America. Another influential house type was derived from a Case Study design by Cliff May (1909–89) and Chris Choate. This was the ranch house, an open-plan single-storey house with floor-to-ceiling windows, which became a definitive Californian house style.

Prefabrication is one of the strategies increasingly adopted to create houses that are not only cheaper and quicker to construct but that also are much more environmentally friendly. In the closed-panel system of timber building, which has been developed to a very high standard in Germany, insulation, internal wall linings and preliminary servicing are installed in the factory. Houses that make use of this type of structural system have excellent thermal performance and a high degree of airtightness. The m-house, a movable house by British architect Tim Pyne, is fully fitted and entirely prefabricated, and is designed to disturb the site as little as possible – a house that leaves no traces.

Case study:
Pawson House

Architect:
John Pawson

Interview with
John Pawson

John Pawson is an internationally acclaimed architect and designer whose work addresses fundamental problems of space, proportion, light and materials. A constant preoccupation is simplicity, or what is often termed 'minimalism'.

Born in Halifax, Yorkshire, in 1949, Pawson spent a formative period in Japan, where he met and was influenced by the Japanese architect and designer Shiro Kuramata (1934–91). After a period of study at the Architectural Association in London, he established his own practice in 1981.

Early commissions included homes for writer Bruce Chatwin, opera director Pierre Audi, contemporary art dealer Hester van Royen and collector Doris Lockhart Saatchi, along with art galleries in London, Dublin and New York. Subsequent projects have been wide-ranging, in both scale and typology, and have included Calvin Klein's flagship store in Manhattan, airport lounges for Cathay Pacific in Hong Kong, the new Cistercian monastery of Our Lady of Nový Dvůr in Bohemia and the Sackler Crossing, a walkway over one of the lakes at Kew's Royal Botanic Gardens.

What's more difficult, designing a house from scratch or reworking an existing one?

Houses that are stand-alone and completely in the round offer the most scope, and therefore they're the most challenging, whereas ones where you're refurbishing an existing structure or mixing old and new may present more complex problems to resolve but you do have a framework to fight against. But every site has restrictions, whether it's nature, views, the client or materials. We always start with a clean sheet and work out the challenges. We like to know about the physical conditions – wind, sun and climate, what the soil is like, and so on. Then we want to look at the culture, history, materials and construction methods. It's all fairly easy stuff to get access to.

Do you find your clients are self-selecting? They know your work and they're coming to you because they want a Pawson house?

Yes, exclusively. Occasionally we get a middle person trying to promote us, but, unless the clients themselves are keen, it's a non-starter. Otherwise you're put in the strange position of selling yourself to someone who may not want what you do. But sometimes we do design for friends and for reasons other than our own aesthetic.

That must rule out a certain degree of friction with the client if they are coming to you for a Pawson house. They've got to have some sort of commitment to living in a particular way.

Yes, but I think you're also dealing with people's dreams. To build a house you need balls. Even the women. It's a long and complicated process. There are exceptions; people do commission and build in a year, but generally it takes much longer. One of the biggest problems is communication. Most people are architects manqué or designers manqué and would like to be doing it themselves. In a way you're there to help them. It's a very collaborative process. All our clients are interesting, dynamic and strong people and I've learned a lot from them. And being a bit older now, I can listen. Most clients have a vision of what they want. They may say, 'We'll wait till John shows us what we can do,' but in their mind they've already formulated an idea and, when you plonk the model down in front of them, it's often completely different from what they thought.

Of course, I think they should agree with me in the end, but often they don't and you have to turn things round. For example, we're doing a house in the woods by a lake in Stockholm, a very inexpensive house for someone who is on a tight budget. I designed what I thought was an exquisite box with a pitched roof in wood. Very simple. But the client was completely deflated because he'd wanted a flat roof and a white box and he got pitched roof and a wood box. And I thought, well, let's talk you through all the reasons why we designed it this way, because everyone here was very happy with it, and two years later he's getting a white box with a flat roof. A lot of my clients are more minimal than I am, they want to live with less and be more rigorous.

If you strip back to that extent you do get something that is more timeless and more eternal...

People always say we like to live outside fashion or that we don't like to be beholden. But I still think you can't avoid being influenced by the present. Everything is touched by time in some way and some things do last better than others. We seem comfortable with the best of Georgian design in England. Quality will out.

There doesn't seem much difference, to be honest, between Roman villas and the present. Glass and steel mean you can do bigger spans with thinner things – you can do big spans uninterrupted with fewer columns – and glass is obviously much larger. Ironmongery has got a bit more sophisticated, but hinges are the same as they were in Roman times and they had underfloor heating, doors, roofs, pantiles and fires. In a way we're going backwards, in the sense that we're returning to that one big room where everything happens. It's what everybody wants in their home regardless of its size or their income.

There's been a tremendous shift in the way people live, hasn't there? No more separate dining rooms.

No, or parlours, or reception rooms. Although it's quite nice to be able to shut a door, I have to say. But my thing has always been to design houses around how I like to live or how my clients like to live. Most people want the same thing.

How would you say the way you like to live affects the design of your houses? That the space is more inclusive?

Yes, and also I don't like too much stuff. I'm also quite analytical. You have to start by thinking about where people are going to gather. We all like a fire and gather round it and we all watch TV and gather round that. Now it's a 63-inch TV, and it may be thin but it's still a very big thing. Chimneys are also big and because they protrude through roofs they have to be considered right at the beginning. Unless people are going to have a dedicated media room, I like to put the two together.

So my first question is always, 'Where are you going to sit and what sort of sofa is it going to be?' and clients usually say, 'Oh don't worry about that, that's the easy bit.' Well, I wouldn't be asking if I thought it was easy. How on earth do you have an elegant comfortable flopping sofa? Because it's a contradiction.

It's the definition of comfortable that is the key one, isn't it?

Well, the irony is that for most people, if a sofa looks comfortable it almost doesn't need to be comfortable. It can be big and puffy with cushions, but if you sit in it for couple of hours to watch a movie you might be really uncomfortable because you're not supported. On the other hand, you might be able to sit in a chair that doesn't look so comfortable and be more comfortable for that period.

It's very important for a space to feel good, which comes from light and proportion, materials and scale, and the way the rooms lead into each other. What's interesting is that when you're designing a church or a chapel, you have to follow the same procedure or the same set of rules, but it has to end up feeling sacred or spiritual. A house doesn't have to be spiritual but it does have to have atmosphere.

I keep telling everybody here you really have to understand how you're going to use every corner, every bit of the house. And question everything. Every place that you sit down should feel good and have nice views, both outside and inside. Things should be a pleasure. Opening and passing through doors, opening cupboards…

Those moments of pleasure are hard to design into a house. You're looking at a lot of detail.

We have designed a door handle and some hinges. And we're also designing a whole system for Bulthaup, which would deal with quite a lot of the house, because it won't just stop at the kitchen; it will include cupboards and other things. But I don't think all the details have to be done by me. It would be a bit much if we designed every single thing.

The furniture you choose is really important, too. You can spoil space by a badly chosen object, which is curious really. I'm not saying that we would have to choose all the furniture either, and we wouldn't, but some types of furnishing or decoration are more successful than others. You need furniture but you don't necessarily need art or found objects on display for a house to have atmosphere. In a way, if you need art, then in some ways you haven't quite got it right. Extraordinary pieces can save you.

What was it like to be your own client? To design your own house?

My house had four clients. Myself, my wife and our two children. You do set yourself up a bit when you design your own house and in a way it's more agonizing. It was Catherine who found the house and bought it. I was in America at the time. It was brilliant because she was able to do all the paperwork without my signature, which was slightly scary too.

When I initially saw the house, I said, 'I'm afraid I can't do anything with this! It's just a London terrace house without a row or terrace.' There were only these two in the street. It was just bunged in like an afterthought.

Why did you think you couldn't do anything with it?

Well, architects like some space widthways. The house has a lot of stairs and its very slim and tall, only 5 metres wide. When you take the stairs off you're not left with much. The footplate's 5 by 8 metres. The house is only 1500 square feet, which is small by Western values, although I suppose it would be big in Japan. Also you can get slightly fed up with the terrace house plan. When you walk into people's houses where they haven't gutted them, you sort of know where things are going to be.

The main point was the site because it's on a communal garden, which was great for the kids. So I could see the potential of that but I just didn't know what I was going to do. In the end it would have been better if I had been allowed to demolish it. It ended up getting completely demolished anyway. The thing about these houses is they're quite adequately made, and they will last two or three hundred years if you don't muck around with them, but everything is the minimum – the beams, brickwork – which you find out as soon as you start to strip them back. I've seen some people remove everything in one go and then the whole back wall falls out. We were obviously quite careful not to do that.

You couldn't touch the front, presumably?

No, we did knock it down and rebuild it, but it's a conservation area. At the back you could do what you wanted to the lower two floors. That's fine, because that's where the vistas are. I was determined to see the extremities of the site. So I'd always say, what's my longest possible option?

I didn't want to try too hard. I did document everything and studied everything that was there before I took anything out. I didn't want to think that I could do better. I could only do different.

How did you start thinking about the new design? Is that something you do in your head or do you start with sketches?

I use sketches to convey to other people what I'm trying to do. With this house, I worked out where I wanted the kitchen to be.

That would fix the relationship with the garden, presumably?

Well, yes. But the thing with the Victorians or Edwardians is that they would dig out a little bit and put it on the road, so you get this half-up half-down business. If you put the kitchen upstairs where the best view is, then what do you use the basement for? And it is a genuine lower ground floor. In the end we put the kitchen down there where it has direct access to the garden and then worked out the other floors. Clearly the first floor ends up by being a sitting area, which means the lower two floors are public and the upper two floors are private.

Where to put the fire and how to do the staircase were other major things. I did a lot of studies on how to make the most economical stair, and I studied the existing plan, of course. Originally, when the house was built, which was 1843, it was a house for a couple with five children and three servants.

Did you research the history?

Tim Knox, who is now at the John Soane Museum, was at the National Trust at the time, and he wrote a history of it for me. Dan Cruickshank came round and felt the bricks. I am obsessional. I also did a survey of what's beneath because we considered having a geothermal heat pump, but didn't because of the disruption to the neighbours and so on. I just liked the idea of having a hot spring.

You explore your ideas and then you limit them to what makes sense for the place. What's very nice about the house is that is has north–south light on all floors, front to back, which is very important to me. Now people are amazed by how big it feels. That's to do with having these vistas, even if they're about looking outside. If you've got a window with a great view, the room can be tiny.

How do you do your thinking? Do you use models?

You cannot do any project, whether it's a table or an interior, without a model. I do sketches, what I would call presentation sketches. We use a software application to do a wire frame model and then I sketch over that. It's to show the scheme but also for me to scribble on.

Did you need to go through that process with this project?

Even more so. I made umpteen models. I needed to keep on correcting things. You obviously do the plan first and then work the three dimensions off the plan. The sections and elevations come quite a bit later and they're more of a check on things. I need two sketches per room so I've got every single surface covered. For this house, that's 36 sketches. You want even the tiniest room to be pleasurable to be in, if possible.

The key things are the fire and TV, where you're going to sit and gather, and the circulation space. Corridor is almost a pejorative term, but you can do beautiful corridors if they have natural light or some sort of gallery. It sounds nicer if you say cloisters or ambulatory. The staircase is hidden but it is a room in its own right, so it's a nice experience going up and down. Obviously, after circulation, storage takes up the most space.

That must come down to quantifying what stuff you've got and measuring it.

No, not really. If you bother to do that, you might as well get rid of it. We've got a lot less than most people, but we've still got more than we need, which is painful for me. It's that business that archivists have to do, which is to evaluate – make a decision about what to keep and what to get rid of – and that's so tiring and difficult; it's easier to just shove it all in a cupboard. Because you're never quite sure if you're going to regret getting rid of something or not. And it's not all my stuff anyway and you can't make judgments for other people.

With storage you tend to build in some flexibility and some variety, so you have narrow shelves and deep shelves and you inevitably compromise because you have to fit the storage in where you can and try not to spoil the room. I don't like to see stuff, but putting doors on does make the rooms a bit narrower. I think I would have less storage now if I could. The cupboard doors are handle-less and white and are supposed to read like a wall, so it can be difficult to tell where things are.

Do you find that you are opening them often to find things?

Yes, and I count them the whole time. I sit in the room going one, two, three, four, five… and of course I know how many there are, but I do this strange thing. I read somewhere or other that it's a sign of stress.

Counting is soothing.

Then I must be stressed. I should stop counting.

Is it easy to live with things stowed away? Or does it become a bit tetchy where you've got to put them back?

No, because you don't put them back unless you want to. They get put back for the photographs. If I'm on my own, which is very rare, I like to clean up. Most of the time stuff doesn't get put back. It's the same sort of Murphy's law with the worktop. Whatever length of worktop you have, it gets filled. Ours is 17 metres long because it goes outside. It's very handy to put things on, but you certainly don't need it to be that long. One area is used for preparation and cooking, another for serving, and there's also a laundry area. I lay out my work on it at the weekend or the evening and the children used to do their homework at it. Now they stand at it reading the newspaper rather irritatingly before dinner. And they put their iPods and things on top. Also they love sitting on it. They even lie on it.

You did have a certain vocabulary to draw on when you were designing this. You knew to some extent what your choices were going to be.

That is true. There are certain givens, which makes it a bit easier. There was only one type of flooring for the house and that was stone, because I wanted to have the stone outside and inside, and in the bathrooms. Of course, there's more than one colour of stone but I wanted the honey-coloured one.

It's a limestone from Lecce in southern Italy. I like limestone because it has fossils in, but it is soft. There is no one material that's perfect. It was used for all the basins, the bench in the living room, the kitchen worktop and the underside of the stairs. It's only used horizontally, except for the bath, where it's vertical, but that counts as furniture.

Normally if you have a bit of time, which we don't have in this day and age, you would like to start from scratch each time. So you would say, what colour are the walls going to be? But of course they are going to be white, although there are lots and lots of shades of white.

Which shade of white do you use?

I use an off-white, which manufacturers call lots of wonderful names like 'quiet white'. I tend to want to take the edge off, which is mainly to do with glare. Some people don't find that pure enough. They say they want white-white, polar white. The reason for using white is obvious – because it's reflective, because it makes the spaces bigger and also you get these wonderful gradations of greys as it changes throughout the day. The house is like a light box: it's extraordinary, it picks up everything, including the light reflected from the terraces. So you get west light in the morning and east light in the evening, which can be a little confusing. I was always worried about the mirrors people put in gardens, but surreptitious use of stainless steel in the future might not be such a bad thing.

The whole end wall of the kitchen is window. How is the glazing detailed?

Two pieces are fixed either side and the middle one slides open, so you can park that. I didn't want there to be a frame. It increases this feeling of inside/outside and I could do that conceit of using the same material inside and out. Blur the boundary. But it blurs it so well that people walk into the glass, which actually I would consider bad design. They tend to walk into the one next to the worktop. Since I've done this, I realize you've got to be careful where you put your picture windows. People don't do it upstairs.

Because they're aware they're on a different level?

Yes, it's like a ha-ha in a garden. People don't normally walk off them for some reason.

How do you get your builders to take so much care? Any mistake is going to jump out at you.

It's terribly unforgiving. If you have floor-to-ceiling doors, ceilings have to be flat; otherwise the doors will catch. If you have cupboards, then you have a series of lines. Not only do you have a grid on the wall, you have a grid on the floor with the stone.

Because it's my own house, I experimented in a way I wouldn't do so much with a client. Or you make it quite clear what you are doing with the client. I didn't make it quite clear to Catherine. I think the thing with building is, unless you're mad, if the builder doesn't get it quite right, you have to be reasonably reasonable. So you have to make a decision whether it really *really* matters and you have to start again, or you have to live with it a bit. And you try and discuss with the builder how you're going to achieve what you want. Again, it's all to do with communication. Most people can achieve what you want if they understand what you're talking about, but they forget – that's the problem. Architects used to be on site all day every day but you can't do that anymore. Anyway, even if you were on site, you'd be on the wrong floor.

Some things are not built for tolerances. Plastering isn't. In a funny way I quite like the fact that certain things move and that the wood behaves naturally and the stone expands and contracts. It's a bit more lived in. When they cut stone, the sword blade's a certain thickness, so you never know if what you're going to get comes from that side or this side of the blade. I thought that when you asked for a 600-millimetre tile that's what you were going to get. Oh, yes, they'd say, give or take. And nothing in my work is give or take. The Japanese can cut and lay stone so perfectly, to unbelievable tolerances. It's gorgeous, but you forget it's natural.

How about the lighting? It's all concealed, is it?

Yes, it's nice not to see the fittings. It's hugely important for atmosphere. There's lots of lighting in coves so it washes the walls and it's also concealed above and below benches. I only put downlights in restricted spaces where they're framed so they're not loose on the ceiling like showers. It makes it difficult to light the table if you do that – that's the problem. We use candles. When you talk about having a vocabulary or certain givens, the walls are white, floors are usually stone or wood or concrete, lighting is concealed, storage is made to disappear.

I suppose it means you can concentrate on bringing out the way different rooms feel.

Even after 12 years I still get huge pleasure every day from waking up in the morning or looking down the stairs or out of the window, or coming down to the kitchen and seeing the quality of the light. The back window often feels like an aquarium because the light is very blue in here in the evening; you could almost think it was a pool.

What about the bathrooms?

I'm not saying this is necessarily right, but I wanted a particularly generous bathroom because you spend more time awake in there than you do in the bedroom. At the top of the house, the roof of the shower in the boys' bathroom slides back electrically so the whole thing is open to the sky. It was expensive to do, but it's nice to have. If you're at the top of the house you might as well have top light.

Do your children share your taste? Do they get what you get out of living in the space?

They've never complained. I think their complaint might be what everyone would say – they'd like a bigger bedroom, but what they really mean is their own space. But interestingly because the whole house is seemingly quite neutral, they're able to colonize. They have no inhibitions about dominating the front room. It's not 'don't touch'. And the TV's there, too.

What do you do with the TV? Do you put it behind a panel?

It's in a cupboard, yes. If the kids are watching TV, we have to retire to bed or we stay in the kitchen. We had to make a choice early on whether we'd be at the top and they'd be lower down, but because they were growing up we didn't want to pass them.

What about the outdoor areas?

As well as the areas front and back, we have a terrace on the first floor. You could eat out up there, but we never do because you have to carry the food up. There's also a roof terrace, which has total privacy and wonderful views, but I didn't quite get the access right. I should have sacrificed some of the bathroom to make a really easy comfortable access.

How long did the house take to build?

Eighteen months. It was a long time. Things do take longer than people think. If builders quoted the real time, they wouldn't get the job. And if they quoted the real money, they wouldn't get the job.

And that's why people get so frustrated with builders, because they can't believe that it's taken twice as long as they said. I know that's as long as it should take, but none of us can say it. Clients always say that if we move in, then they'll get the message and hurry. But builders don't want to hang around longer than they have to. Building's just a very imprecise business.

One of the strange things is that architecture is really about interiors. All these architects say 'I'm not a decorator', as if there's some hierarchy. Occasionally we'll get introduced to people as decorators, which is what I do anyway, and I'm always happy to see what I can learn. You can't possibly do a building without thinking about the interior – I'm not saying you have to be a dab hand at carpets and curtains – but you need to know where furniture is going to go, you need to know how people are going to use the rooms. Really what people want to see is how you make space.

Pawson House, 1999

Below: The staircase
is an evocative element
of the design, the result of
extensive studies into the
most economical use of space.

Right: Sketch of the rear
elevation showing the
worktop extending the
length of the kitchen and
out into the garden.

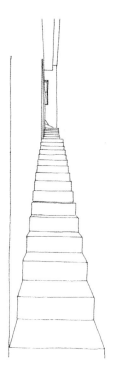

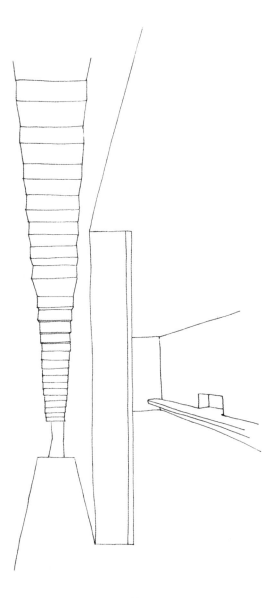

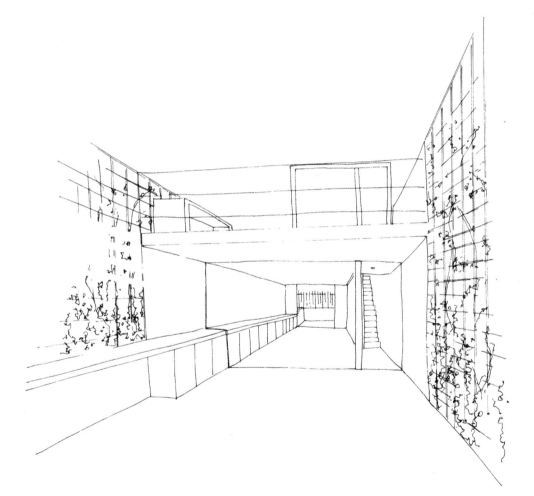

The rear elevation of the
Pawson House. Unifying
interior and exterior is a
17-metre-long worktop made
of Italian limestone, the same
material used as flooring.
All lighting is concealed.

The lower ground floor is entirely given over to a kitchen/eating area. One area of the worktop is used for preparation and cooking, another for serving and another for laundry.

The end wall of the kitchen is entirely glazed and is composed of three floor-to-ceiling sections of glass. The outer two sections are fixed in position, while the middle section slides open and across.

The living room on the
first floor and the staircase
viewed from the entrance.
The same vocabulary
was used throughout the
house: limestone flooring,
white walls.

The living room on the first floor with the Pawson-designed 'sofadesk' (manufactured by Driade). All storage in the house is concealed in seamless cupboards.

Left: At the top of the house a glazed slot running the length of the ceiling allows light to spill down the triple-height staircase.

Right: The children's rooms are at the top of the house and lead off a shared workspace.

This spread and over: Because the house is in a conservation area in west London, planning regulations prohibited alterations to the front elevation. Behind the façade, however, floor layouts were radically reworked to give the maximum amount of free space and natural light.

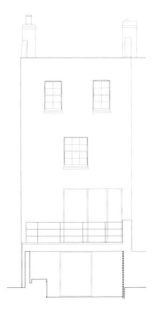

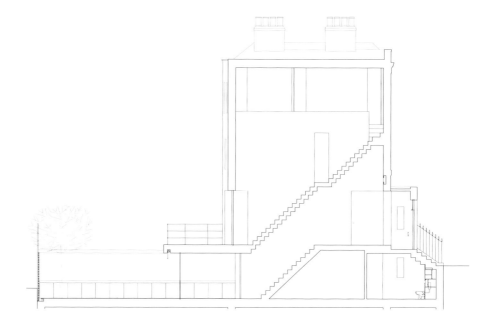

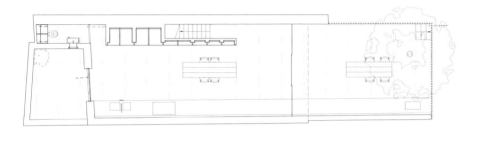

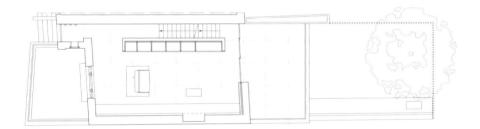

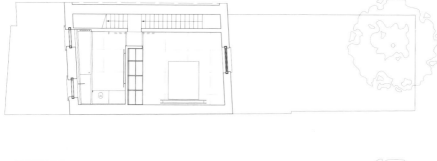

Selected works

Architect:
John Pawson

Nový Dvůr Monastery
Czech Republic, 2004

From a house for a family
to a house for a whole
community. In 1999 John
Pawson was commissioned
by the Trappist Order of
monks to design a new
monastery on a site west
of Prague. The scheme
combined elements of an
old baroque manor house
and its outbuildings with
new architecture. At the
heart of the new complex is
the monastery church of
Our Lady, which in its rigorous,
crisp form reflects the austere
ethics and lifestyle of the
20 or so Trappist monks
who live in the community.

Nový Dvůr

Below: The monastery forecourt. The design, with its emphasis on the quality of light and proportion, simple, pared-down elevations and detailing, remains true to the spiritual preoccupations of the Order.

Right: The chapel interior shows a characteristically restrained palette of plaster, concrete, timber and glass. The play of light animates the architecture and adds precision, drama and mystery to the experience of space.

Tetsuka House
Tokyo, 2005

This design for a compact
house in Tokyo takes the
form of a pristine box,
containing living quarters,
a tearoom and a courtyard
open to the sky. Openings cut
into the concrete structure
frame a series of vistas.

Sackler Crossing
Royal Botanic Gardens,
Kew, 2006

This bridge across the lake at Kew takes the form of a serpentine path, with the deck set at the minimum possible distance from the lake's surface, to allow those crossing to feel as if they are walking on water. Glimpses through the deck treads and the barely visible supporting steel structure enhance this quality. Bands of dark granite laid like railway sleepers form the deck; cast bronze vertical cantilevers set between the treads serve as balusters. Viewed end on, they read as a solid construction; from the side the solidity fragments, allowing views through.

Index

Glossary

Arts and Crafts movement
Nineteenth-century design
movement pioneered by
William Morris that sought
to reconnect with traditional
(pre-industrial) British crafts,
materials and values.

brutalism A stark, vigorous
development of modernism
characteristic of the 1950s
and 1960s.

classical orders One of
the predominant styles of
ancient Greek and Roman
architecture. The styles –
most recognizable in the kind
of column deployed – were
the Tuscan, Ionic, Corinthian,
Doric and Composite.

classicism A style of
architecture developed
during the Renaissance
that looked back to the
architectural achievements
of ancient Greece and
Rome and that privileged
the ideals of proportion,
symmetry and order.

De Stijl An early twentieth-
century Dutch movement in
art, design and architecture,
founded in 1917, that married
the modernist tenets of
harmony and order with
a concern for the spiritual.
In domestic architecture its
iconic high point was the
Rietveld Schröder House
in Utrecht, built in 1924.

elevation A scale drawing
showing the vertical
projection of one side of
a building.

envelope The outer shell
of a building, providing
environmental protection
and structural integrity.

façade The 'face' of the
house – the interface between
the private and public, the
domestic and civic.

earth-sheltering Where
houses are partially or almost
entirely covered by the ground,
making use of the fact that
earth gains and loses heat
much more slowly than the air.

Ionic One of the classical
orders, characterized by scroll
shapes on either side of the
capital (head) of the column.

machiya Timber-framed
townhouse traditional to
Japanese vernacular
architecture, found throughout
Japan and especially Kyoto.

Minimalism A style of
architecture, first developed
in the post–World War II
period, that rigorously applies
the tenets of modernism.

Modernism An early
twentiethth-century movement
in architecture that rejected
applied style and decoration
and placed the emphasis
on function, the free flow
of space, light and air and
the use of modern materials
and structural methods.

open (free) plan The free
flow of space in the plan of
house, with no or very few
dividing walls.

passive solar strategies
The exploitation of site
and design to maximize
a building's energy
efficiency (e.g. through
solar orientation), contrasted
with 'active' strategies such
as photovoltaics.

pilaster A rectangular
column.

piloti In modern architecture,
columns or stilts that raise a
building above ground level,
creating an open circulation
space beneath.

plan A scale drawing of
the horizontal projection
of a building.

prefabrication The practice
of producing (usually
standardized) architectural
components in a factory
or workshop and
subsequently assembling
on site to create the finished
building.

ribbon window A window in
a continuous horizontal band,
structured by a series of
vertical posts, or mullions.

rustication A style of masonry
featuring large blocks, deep
joints and a roughened
surface.

wattle and daub The classic
materials of domestic
medieval houses. Wattle
is the woven framework of
stakes, branches and twigs;
daub, the insulating covering
of mud or clay.

Picture credits

The publisher would like to thank the following photographers and agencies for their kind permission to reproduce the following photographs:

Front cover Margherita Spiluttini

2 © J.Paul Getty Trust. Used with permission. Julius Shulman Photography Archive, Research Library at the Getty Research Institute (2004.R.10); 7 Margherita Spiluttini; 8 NTPL/Andrew Butler; 9 Charlotte Wood/ Arcaid; 10 Werner Forman/ Arcaid; 11 Werner Forman Archive; 12 ©The National Gallery, London; 14 Ellen Rooney/Robert Harding Picture Library/Alamy; 17 Alvar Aalto Museum; 18 W&D Downey/Getty Images; 19 above Nigel Young; 19 below Make Architects; 20 above Max Dupain & Associates; 20 below The Estate of R. Buckminster Fuller; 22-23 Ushida Findlay Architects; 24-25 Richard Davies; 27 Edifice/The Bridgeman Art Library; 28 ©2009. The Frank Lloyd Wright Fdn, AZ/Art Resource, NY/Scala, Florence; 29 ©2009. Digital image Mies van der Rohe/ Gift of the Arch./MoMA/Scala, Florence; 30 Thomas A Heinz/Arcaid; 31 Avery Architectural & Fine Arts Library; 32 below left John Donat/RIBA Library Photographs Collection; 32 below right & above RIBA Library Photographs Collection; 33 John Dominis/ Time Life Pictures/Getty Images; 34-35 Peter Cook/ VIEW; 36 Hans Werlemann; 37 Office for Metropolitan Architecture; 38 Werner Forman/Arcaid; 39 Natalie Tepper/Arcaid; 40 Philippa Lewis/Edifice/Arcaid; 41 above JTB Photo Communications Inc/Alamy; 41 below Paola Negri/Alamy; 42-43 Hiroyuki Hirai; 44 above AEP/Alamy; 44 below Patrice Latron/Corbis; 46 RIBA Library Photographs Collections; 48-49 National Maritime Museum; 50 above Schutze/Rodemann/Bildarchi v Monheim GmbH/Alamy ©FLC/ADAGP, Paris and DACS, London 2010; 50 below Adrian Forty/Edifice /Corbis ©FLC/ADAGP, Paris and DACS, London 2010; 52 Fondation le Corbusier ©FLC/ADAGP, Paris and DACS, London 2010; 53 Emilio Suetone/Hemis/ Alamy ©FLC/ADAGP, Paris and DACS, London 2010; 54 Phil Wills/Alamy; 57 above left Michael Halberstadt/ Arcaid/Alamy; 57 below Bill Maris/ESTO/Arcaid; 57 above right Michael Halberstadt/ Arcaid; 58 Klaus Frahm/Artur/ VIEW; 60 Alan Weintraub/ Arcaid; 63 Felix Borkenau; 64 Tim Street-Porter; 67 Hisao Suzuki; 82-83 John Pawson; 84-85 Hisao Suzuki; 86-95 Richard Glover/VIEW; 96-99 John Pawson; 101–103 Richard Glover/VIEW; 104-105 Hisao Suzuki; 106 Richard Glover/VIEW; 107 Edmund Sumner/VIEW.

Every effort has been made to trace the copyright holders. We apologise in advance for any unintentional omissions and would be pleased to insert the appropriate acknowledgement in any subsequent publication.

Credits

First published in 2010
by Conran Octopus Ltd
in association with
The Design Museum

Conran Octopus,
a part of Octopus Publishing
Group, Endeavour House,
189 Shaftesbury Avenue,
London WC2H 8JY
www.octopusbooks.co.uk

A Hachette UK Company
www.hachette.co.uk

Distributed in the United
States and Canada by
Hachette Book Group USA,
237 Park Avenue, New York,
NY 10017 USA

British Library Cataloguing-
in-Publication Data.
A catalogue record for
this book is available
from the British Library.

Text written by:
Elizabeth Wilhide

Publisher:
Lorraine Dickey
Consultant Editor:
Deyan Sudjic
Managing Editor:
Sybella Marlow
Editor:
Robert Anderson

Art Director:
Jonathan Christie
Design:
Untitled
Picture Researcher:
Anne-Marie Hoines

Production Manager:
Katherine Hockley

ISBN: 978 1 84091 545 7
Printed in China